# The Origin And Objects Of Ancient Freemasonry: Its Introduction Into The United States, And Legitimacy Among Colored Men

Martin Robison Delany

THE

# ORIGIN AND OBJECTS

OF

# ANCIENT FREEMASONRY;

ITS

INTRODUCTION INTO THE UNITED STATES,

AND

# LEGITIMACY AMONG COLORED MEN.

A TREATISE DELIVERED BEFORE

St. Cyprian Lodge, No 13, June 24th, A. D. 1853----A. L. 5853.

BY

M. R. DELANY, K. M., D. D. G. H P.

"Great is Truth, and must prevail."

PITTSBURGH:

PRINTED BY W. S. HAVEN, CORNER MARKET AND SECOND STREETS.

1853.

Soc 7850.5

1854. April 24.
Gift of Alexander H. [illegible], Esq.
[illegible]

Entered according to Act of Congress, in the year 1853, by
M. R. DELANY,
In the Clerk's Office of the District Court of the Western District of Pennsylvania.

THIS LITTLE TREATISE

IS MOST RESPECTFULLY DEDICATED

TO THE

MASONIC FRATERNITY

THROUGHOUT THE WORLD,

BY THE AUTHOR.

# CORRESPONDENCE.

PITTSBURGH, June 27, A. D. 1853, A. L. 5853.

*Brother Martin R. Delany:*

SIR—The undersigned have been appointed
a Committee from St. Cyprian Lodge, No. 13, of A. Y. Masons,
to solicit the Treatise delivered by you on the 24th of June, A. D.
1853, A. L. 5853, for publication in pamphlet form, hoping thereby to subserve the cause of the Craft generally, and that of the
Colored Masons in the United States in particular.

Such a dissertation on Masonry has long been needed to set
the public mind, and that of the unskilled in the Craft, right on
several important and essential points in Masonic jurisprudence,
and we are fully assured that in your Treatise, this has been ac
complished.

With high regard, fraternally yours,

ELIAS EDMONDS,
THOMAS NORRIS,
W. J. TRUSTY.

PITTSBURGH, June 30, A. D. 1853, A. L. 5853.

*Companion and Sir Knight:*

The undersigned, by a resolution of a
Grand Lodge Communication, were appointed a Committee to
solicit, in conjunction with a Committee from St. Cyprian Lodge,
No. 13, a copy of the able Treatise delivered by you on the occasion of the last Annual Festival of St. John the Baptist. We
take pleasure in uniting our own with the sentiments contained
in the above note, and hope ever to remain

Yours, in the ties of Fraternal esteem,

WM. B. AUSTIN, D. D. G. M.
ALFRED H. JOHNS,
JAMES GRIGG,
FRANCIS J. HALL,
JONATHAN GREEN.

1*

PITTSBURGH, June 30, A. D. 1853, A. L. 5853.

*Gentlemen, Brethren, Companions and Sir Knights:*

I have received a note jointly from a Committee appointed by St. Cyprian Lodge, No. 13, and a Communication held by the District Deputy Grand Master, desiring that the Treatise delivered by me before the public, on the 24th day of June inst. (the Annual Festival of our Patron, St. John the Baptist,) be published in pamphlet form. With this request, I readily and cheerfully comply.

Permit me to say, in this connection, that whatever undue and unwarrantable obstructions may be thrown in our way by *American* Masons; and they are many—though there are *some* honorable exceptions—it is within the power of the Grand Lodge of England to decide in the matter, and at once establish our *validity*. For this purpose, I now suggest, through you, that all of our Subordinate Lodges throughout the United States, at once petition their respective Grand Lodges, and the Grand Lodges respectively agree, and, together with the National Grand Lodge, meet by delegated representatives of *Past Masters*—not to exceed three from each Grand Lodge, and the same number from each District over which there may be a District Deputy Grand Master; the National Grand Lodge sending *one* for each *State Grand Lodge*—in a National Grand Masonic Convention, for the single purpose of petitioning the Grand Lodge of England for a *settlement* of the question of the *legality of Colored Masons in the United States,* claiming to have originated from the warrant granted to Prince Hall, of Boston. This should at once be done, to settle the controversy, as it would to us be a great point gained, because it would be the acknowledgment and establishment of a *right* among us as a people, which is now *disputed*, but which *legitimately* belongs to us.

We have for years been fraternally outraged, simply for the want of a proper and judicious course being pursued on the part of *our* Masonic authorities, and the present loudly calls upon us for action in this matter. We are either Masons or not Masons, legitimate or illegitimate; if the affirmative, then we *must* be so *acknowledged* and *accepted*—if the negative, we *should* be *rejected*. We never will relinquish a claim to an everlasting inheritance, but by the force of stern necessity; and there is not that Masonic power in existence, with the exception of the Grand Lodge of England, to which we will yield in a decision on this point. Our rights are equal to those of other American Masons, if not better than some; and it comes not with the best grace for *them* to *deny* us.

The suggested Convention should be held in some central place, during the ensuing three years of the National Grand Lodge administration, and in not less than one year from this date, so that full time may be given, for reflection and action, on the part of the various Subordinate and Grand Lodges.

Let not the hopes of our brethren languish, though calumny and slander may have done their work.

> O, Slander! foulest imp of hell!
>  Thy tongue is like the scorpion's sting!
> Nor peace nor hope can near thee dwell;
>  Thy breath can blast the fairest thing!
> O, could I grasp the thunderbolt!
>  I'd crush thee, limping fiend of hell!
> From earth I'd chase thy serpent soul,
>  And chain thee where the furies dwell!
>
> BISHOP PAYNE.

Fraternally Yours,

In the bonds of Union and Fellowship,

M. R. DELANY.

To ELIAS EDMONDS, WM. B. AUSTIN, &c. *Committees.*

# A TREATISE.

"Great is Truth, and must prevail."

To introduce the subject of Ancient Freemasonry at this period, with a design to adduce anything new, at least to the enlightened, would be a work of supererogation, having the semblance of assumption, more than an effort to impart information.

Summoned by your invitation to deliver a Treatise, I have chosen for my subject, The Origin, Objects, and Introduction of Freemasonry into the United States—and also its introduction among colored men in this country. I shall, therefore, proceed at once to the discharge of my duty, doing the best I can according to the opportunity and means at hand for the accomplishment of this end.

Masonry was originally intended for the better government of man—for the purpose of restraining him from a breach of the established ordinances. The first law given to man was by God himself—that given in the Garden of Eden, forbidding the eating of the reserved fruit. (Gen. 2:17.) The first institution was that of marriage. (Gen. 2:21, 24.) The first breach of the law was committed by eating the forbidden fruit. (Gen. 3:6.) The first punishment inflicted on man was by God himself, for a breach of the law. (Gen. 3:16–19.) The first city was built by Cain, and named after his first-born son, Enoch.

### MAN FROM ADAM TO NOAH.

During the period from Adam to Noah, the life of man was of long duration, each individual living through several hundred years of time. His habits, customs and manner of living were simple; residing in thinly peopled localities, for there were then no densely populated cities, and relying mainly on husbandry as a means of support.

### MAN FROM NOAH TO SOLOMON.

From Noah to Solomon, the character of man underwent an entire and important change. Noah's three sons, scattering abroad over the earth, built great cities, and established many and various policies, habits, manners and customs, for the government of their people. At this period, it will be remembered, a general separation in interests and sympathies took place among these brethren, (the children of one household parentage,) which continued to manifest itself in hostile array until the building of the temple by Solomon, king of Israel. I do not pretend to assert that hostilities then entirely ceased, but that mankind were better governed after that period, will not be denied.

In the earliest period of the Egyptian and Ethiopian dynasties, the institution of Masonry was first established. Discovering a defect in the government of man, first suggested an inquiry into his true state and condition. Being a people of a high order of intellect, and subject to erudite and profound thought, the Egyptians and Ethiopians were the first who came to the conclusion that man was created in the similitude of God. This, it will be remembered, was anterior to the Bible record, because Moses was the recorder of the Bible, subsequent to his exodus from Egypt, all his wisdom and ability having been acquired there; as a proof of which, the greatest recommendation to his fitness for so high and holy an office, and the best encomium wh'ch that book can possibly bestow upon him in testimony of his qualifications as its scriptor, the Bible itself tells us that "Moses was learned in all the *wisdom* of the Egyptians."

The Ethiopians early adduced the doctrine and believed in a trinity of the Godhead. Though heathens, their mythology was of a high and pure order, agreeing in regard to the attributes of the Deity with the doctrine of Christians in after ages, as is beautifully illustrated in the person of Jupiter Ammon, the great god of Egypt and Ethiopia, who was assigned a power over heaven, earth and hell, as well as over all the other gods, thereby acknowledging his omnipotence—all other gods possessing but one divine attribute or function, which could only be exercised in his particular department of divinity.\*

### MAN THE LIKENESS OF GOD.

What is God, that man should be his image, and what knowledge should man obtain in order to be like God? This wisdom was possessed in the remotest period by the wise men of Egypt and Ethiopia, and handed down only through the priesthood to the recipients of their favors, the mass of mankind being ignorant of their own nature, and

\* Jupiter was represented as seated on a throne of gold and ivory—figurative of heaven, as the "pearly gates and golden streets,"—holding in his left hand a sceptre, figurative of his earthly power: his right hand grasping a thunder-bolt, the ancient idea of the power and terrors of hell.

consequently prone to rebel against their greatest and best interests.

God is a being possessing various attributes: and all Masons, whether Unitarian, Trinitarian, Greek, Jew or Mohammedan, agree upon this point, at least without controversy. Where there are various functions, there must be an organ for the exercise of each function,—and this conclusion most naturally led man to inquire into his own nature, to discover the similitude between himself and his Creator.

The three great attributes of Deity—all-wise, omnipotence, and omnipresence—were recognized by the ancients, and represented in the character given to their ruling god —as above mentioned—as presiding over the universe of eternal space—of *celum*, *terra*, and *tartarus*—answering to the Christian doctrine of three persons in one—Father, Son and Holy Ghost.*

Man, then, to assimilate God, must, in his nature, be a trinity of systems—morally, intellectually and physically. This great truth appears to have been known to King David, who, with emotion, exclaims, "We are wonderfully and fearfully made."

To convince man of the importance of his own being, and impress him with a proper sense of his duty to his Creator, were what was desired, and to effect this, would

---

* One of the old doctrines of the priesthood was, that God the Father presided over heaven, the Holy Ghost on earth, and Christ the Son in hell; hence, his descent into the grave, is called a descent into hell, where some believe, or affect to believe, he ever remains: and this is the foundation of the belief of that Christian sect whose doctrines teach a purification and redemption in the grave,—purgatory, a place of purging or purification— or hell.

also impress him with a sense of his duty and obligations to society and the laws intended for his government. For this purpose, was the beautiful fabric of Masonry established, and illustrated in the structure of man's person.

Man, scientifically developed, is a moral, intellectual and physical being—composed of an osseous, muscular and vital structure; of solid, flexible and liquid parts. With an intellect—a mind, the constituent principles of which he is incapable of analyzing or comprehending; which rises superior to its earthy tenement; with the velocity of lightning, soars to the summit of altitude, descends to the depth of profundity, and flies to the wide-spread expanse of eternal space. What can be more God-like than this, to understand which is to give man a proper sense of his own importance, and consequently his duty to his fellows, by which alone, he fulfills the high mission for which he was sent on his temporary pilgrimage.

While the Africans, who were the authors of this mysterious and beautiful Order, did much to bring it to perfection by the establishment of the great principles of man's likeness to Jehovah in a triune existence; yet, until the time of King Solomon, there was a great deficiency in his government, in consequence of the policy being monopolized by the priesthood and certain privileged classes or families.

### FROM SOLOMON DOWN.

For the purpose of remedying what was now conceived to be a great evil in the policy of the world, and for their better government to place wisdom within the acquirement of all men, King Solomon summoned together the united wisdom of the world,—men of all nations and races—to consider the great project of reducing the mystic ties to a more practical and systematic principle, and stereotyping it with physical science, by rearing the stupendous and magnificent temple at Jerusalem.* For the accomplishment of this masterpiece of all human projects, there were laborers or attendants, mechanics or workmen, and overseers or master-builders. Added to these, there was a designer or originator of all the schemes, an architect or draughtsman, and a furnisher of all the materials for the building—all and every thing of which was classified and arranged after the order of trinity, the building itself, when finished, being composed of an outer, an inner, and a central court.

After the completion of this great work, the implements of labor having been laid aside, there were scattered to the utmost parts of the earth, seventy thousand laborers, eighty thousand workmen, and three thousand and three

* Previous to the building of the temple, Masonry was only allegorical, consisting in a scientific system of theories, taught through the medium of Egyptian, Ethiopian, Assyrian, and other oriental hieroglyphics, understood only by the priesthood and a chosen few. All the sovereigns and members of the royal families were Masons, because each member of the royal household had of necessity to be educated in the rituals of the priesthood. And it was not until after Masonry was introduced into Asia by the Jews—it being strictly forbidden by the Jewish laws for women to be priests—that females were prohibited from being Masons. Among other nations of the ancients, priestesses were common, as is known to the erudite in history; and Candace, queen of Sheba, was a high-priestess in her realm—hence her ability to meet King Solomon in the temple, having passed the guards. by the words of wisdom, from the outer to the inner court, where she met the king in all his wisdom, power and glory.

hundred master-builders, making one hundred and fifty-three thousand and three hundred artizans,* each of whom having been instructed in all the mysteries of the temple, was fully competent to teach all the arts and sciences acquired at Jerusalem in as many different cities, provinces, states or tribes. At this period, the mysteries assumed the name of Masonry, induced from the building of the temple; and at this time, also, commenced the universality of the Order, arising from the going forth of the builders into all parts of the world. This, then, was the *establishment of Masonry*, which has been handed down through all succeeding ages.

For a period of years after the destruction of the temple and the sacred or mystic records, there was some slight derangement in the Craft; men were becoming ungovernable both in church and state, owing to the want of proper instruction, and their consequent ignorance of the relation they bore to their Creator and society. For the purpose of again bringing back the "prodigal son" to the household of his father, the "stray sheep" to the rich pastures of the fold of Israel, and repairing the somewhat defaced honored monument of time, Prince Edwin of England, in 930 of the Christian era, being nine hundred and twenty-two years ago, summoned together at York, all the wise men of the order, where the rites were again scientifically systematized, and preserved for coming time. At this point, the Order, in honor to Prince Edwin, assigned to itself the title of *York Masonry*.

* Here the Trinity is again typified: *three times* fifty thousand, *three times* one thousand, and *three times* one hundred.

16

## THE STAGES OF MAN'S HISTORY.

We have here the history of man's existence from Adam to Solomon, showing three distinct periods, fraught with more mystery than all things else, save the ushering in of the Christian era by the birth of the adorable Son of God: his origin in Adam's creation, his preservation in Noah's ark, and his prospects of redemption from the curse of God's broken laws by the promises held out in that mysteriously incomprehensible work of building the temple by Solomon. Adam, Noah and Solomon, then, are the three great types of the condition of man—his sojourn here on earth, and his prospects of a future bliss.

Founded upon the similitude and consequent responsibility to his Creator, the ancients taught the doctrine of a rectitude of conduct and purpose of heart, as the only surety for the successful government of man, and the regulations of society around him. Whether Gentiles, Greeks or Jews, all taught the same as necessary to his government on earth—his responsibility to a Supreme Being, the author and creator of himself. But the mythology of those days, not unlike the scientific theology of the days in which we live, consisted of a sea of such metaphysical depth, that the mass of mankind was unable to fathom it. Instead, then, of accomplishing the object for which this wise policy was established, the design was thwarted by the manner in which it was propagated. Man adhered but little, and cared less, for that in which he could never be fully instructed, nor be made to understand, in consequence of his deficiency in a thorough literary education—this being the exclusive privilege of those in affluent circumstances. All these imperfections have been remedied, in the practical workings of the comprehensive system of Free and Accepted Masonry, as handed down to us from the archives at Jerusalem. All men, of every country, clime, color and condition, (when morally worthy,) are acceptable to the portals of Masonic jurisprudence.

In many parts of the world, the people of various nations were subject to lose their liberty in several ways. A forfeiture by crime, as in our country; by voluntary servitude for a stipulated sum or reward, as among the Hindoos; and by capture in battle and being sold into slavery, as in Algiers. Against these Masonry found it necessary to provide, and accordingly, the first two classes were positively proscribed as utterly unworthy of its benefits, as they were equally unworthy of the respectful consideration of the good among mankind. In this, however, was never contemplated the third class of bondees; for none but he who *voluntarily* compromised his liberty was recognized as a slave by Masons. As there must be a criminal intention in the commission of a crime, so must the act of the criminal be voluntary; hence the criminal and the voluntary bondsman have both forfeited their Masonic rights by willing degradation. In the case of the captive, an entirely different person is presented before us, who has greater claims upon our sympathies than the untrammeled freeman. Instead of the degraded vassal and voluntary slave, whose prostrate position only facilitates the aspect of his horrible deformity, you have the bold, the brave, the high-minded, the independent-spirited, and manly form of a kindred brother in humanity, whose heart is burning, whose breast is heaving, and whose soul is wrung with panting aspirations for liberty—a commander, a chieftain, a knight, or a prince, it may be—still he is a captive, and by the laws of captivity a slave. Does Masonry, then, comtemplate the withholding of its privileges from such applicants as these? Certainly not; since Moses, (to whom our great Grand Master Solomon, the founder of the temple, is indebted for his Masonic wisdom,) was born and lived in captivity eighty years, and by the laws of his captors a slave. It matters not whether captured in actual conflict, sleeping by the wayside, or in a cradle of bulrushes, after birth; so that there be a longing aspiration for liberty, and a manly determination to be free. Policy alone will not permit of the order to confer Masonic privileges on one while yet in captivity; but the fact of his *former* condition as such, or that of his parents, can have no bearing whatever on him. The *mind* and *desires* of the recipient must be *free;* and at the *time* of his endowment with these privileges, his *person* and mind must be unencumbered with all earthly trammels or fetters. This is what is meant by Free and Accepted Masonry, to distinguish it from the order when formerly conferred upon the few, like the order of nobility, taking precedence by rank and birth, whether the inheritor was worthy or not of so high and precious privileges.

In the three great periods as presented to view, you have the three great stages of man's existence—Adam, with child-like innocence in the Garden of Eden, turned out for disobedience, as a youth upon the world without the protecting hand of his Omnipotent Parent—Noah, as in adventurous manhood, in constructing and launching his great vessel (the Ark) upon the "face of the great deep;" and Solomon, as in old age, in devising, planning and counseling, and heaping up treasures in building the Temple of Jerusalem; all of which is impressively typified.

in the cardinal Degrees of Masonry. The Entered Apprentice as a child, and as in youth the Fellow Craft; the Master Mason, as in mature and thinking manhood; and as an old and reflective man of years and wisdom, the Royal Arch completes the history of his journey of life.

ITS INTRODUCTION INTO THE UNITED STATES.

Masonry was introduced into the United States by grant of a warrant to Henry Price, Esq. of Boston, on the 30th of July, 1733, as Right Worshipful Grand Master of North America, "with full power and authority to appoint his Deputy," by the Right Honorable and Most Worshipful Anthony Lord Viscount Montague, "Grand Master of Masons in England." *Cole's Lib. p.* 332. I do not conceive it necessary to prosecute the history of Masonry farther in this country; but let it suffice to say, that hostilities which commenced between Great Britain and America in 1775, absolved all Masonic ties between the two countries, and left American Masons free to act according to the suggestions of the peculiar circumstances in which they were then placed. With the independence of the country, commenced the independence of Masonic jurisdiction in the United States.*

* It is said, that at that early period of its existence in this country, entertaining a kind of superstitious idea of its sacredness, the Masonic warrant was kept closely in some secret place, prohibited from the view of all but Masons; consequently, when General Warren—who was the Grand Master of Massachusetts—fell in the Revolutionary struggle, the warrant was lost, and with it, Masonry in Massachusetts. All Masons are familiar with the fact, that Grand Master Warren was *raised* from his grave and a *search* made, doubtless, supposing that the warrant might have been found concealed about his person.

The Grand Lodge of Massachusetts was formed in 1769; Maine, New Hampshire, 1789; Rhode Island, 1791; Vermont, 1794; New York, 1787; (another being established in 1826, which has recently been denounced by England and all other legal Masonic jurisdictions throughout the world;) New Jersey, 1786; Pennsylvania, 1734, under England, to which she remained attached until September, 1786, when the connection was absolved; Delaware, 1806; Virginia, 1778; N. Carolina, 1787; S. Carolina, 1787; Georgia, 1786; Ohio, 1808; Kentucky, 1800; Louisiana, Mississippi and Tennessee, the data not being given. *Cole's Lib. pp.* 363 *to* 375. This gives a fair history of the introduction of Masonry into the United States of America.

### AMONG COLORED MEN IN THE UNITED STATES.

In the year 178—, a number of colored men in Boston, Massachusetts, applied to the proper source for a grant of Masonic privileges, which being denied them, by force of necessity they went to England, which, at that time not recognizing the Masonic fraternity of America, the then acting Grand Master, (recorded on the warrant as the Right Honorable, Henry Frederick, Duke of Cumberland) granted a warrant to the colored men to make Masons and establish Lodges, subject, of course, to the Grand Lodge of England. In course of time, their ties became absolved; not before it was preceded by the establishment of an independent Grand Lodge in Philadelphia, Pa., by colored men, and subsequently, a general Grand Lodge, known as the First Independent African Grand Lodge of North America.

In the year 1832, another Grand Lodge was established by a party of dissatisfied colored Masons in the city of Philadelphia, known as the "Hiram Grand Lodge of the

State of Pennsylvania."* There was, also, for many years,
a small faction who rather opposed the F. I. A. G. L. still
adhering to what they conceived to be the most legitimate
source—tne old African Lodge of Boston; among whom
was the colored Lodge of Boston, and a very respectable
body in New York city, known as the "Boyer Lodge."
In December, 1847, by a grand communication of a repre-
sentative body of all the colored Lodges in the United
States, held in the city of New York, the differences and
wounds which long existed were all settled and healed, a
complete union formed, and a National Grand Lodge established, by the choice and election, in due Masonic form,
of Past Master, John T. Hilton, of Boston, Mass. Most
Worshipful Grand Master of the National Grand Lodge,
and William E. Ambush, M. W. N. G. Secretary. This,
perhaps, was the most important period in the history of
colored Masons in the United States; and had I the power
to do so, I would raise my voice in tones of thunder, but
with the pathetic affections of a brother, and thrill the cord
of every true Masonic heart throughout the country and
the world; especially of colored men; in exhortations to
stability and to Union. Without it, satisfied am I, that
all our efforts, whether as men or Masons, must fail—utterly fail. "A house divided against itself, cannot stand"—
the weak divided among themselves in the midst of the
mighty, are thrice vanquished—conquered without a blow
from the strong; the sturdy hand of the ruthless may

* This Grand Lodge dissolved in 1847, after an existence of
fifteen years, becoming convinced that they had no just nor legal
foundation for an independent existence; and none contributed
more to the accomplishment of so desirable an end, than the then
acting Grand Master of the Hiram Grand Lodge,—Mr. Samue
Van Brakle, an upright, intelligent, and excellent man.

shatter in pieces our column guidance, and leave the Virgin of Sympathy to weep through all coming time.

I have thus, as cursorily as possible, given you a faint history of the origin and objects of ancient Free Masonry; its introduction into this country among white and colored men; and he who rejects Masonry as an absurd and irreligious institution, must object to the Scriptures of eternal truth, and spurn the Bible as a book of mummeries.

But there have been serious objections urged against the legitimacy of Ancient Freemasonry among *colored* men of African descent or affinity in the United States, eminating at various times from different directions, of high Masonic authority in the Republic, and, consequently, received and adopted with a readiness as surprising as it was unkind and unjust by almost all of the Subordinate, and many of the Grand Lodges throughout the country, especially in the non-slaveholding States.*

Among the earliest, and, peradventure, the first of these intended fratricidal assaults, was that of the Grand Lodge of Pennsylvania in the year 18—; a distinguished and talented ex-editor and present member of Congress, and Col.

*A fact worthy of remark, that there is no comparison between the feelings manifested toward colored, by Northern and Southern Masons. Northern Masons, notwithstanding Masonry knows no man by descent, origin, or color, seldom visit colored Masonic Lodges; and when they do, it is frequently done by *stealth!* While, to the contrary, Southern Masons recognize and fellowship colored men, as such, whenever they meet them as Masons. The writer has more than once sat in Lodge in the city of C——, with some of the first gentlemen of Kentucky, where there have been present Col. A. a distinguished lawyer, Esquire L. one of the first Aldermen of the place, and Judge M. President of the Judges' Bench. This is a matter of no unfrequent occurrence, and many of our members have done the same.

P. an ex-Post Master, if I mistake not, being at the time among the Grand Officers, if not the Committee who visited and reported concerning the African Grand Lodge in Eleventh Street, Philadelphia. And I should not at this late day refer to the doings of those distinguished personages in this connection, but for the purpose of—as it never as yet has publicly been done—vindicating the above named First Independent African Grand Lodge of North America, against the aspersions of those multifarious outward forces which have so long been leveled against her Masonic ramparts. Lambparts, perhaps, would be a term far more appropriate; because our Masonic fathers have submitted really with the most lamb-like passiveness to the terrible and disparaging ordeal.

In this wise, the circumstance referred to happened. The question had long been mooted among the white members of the Fraternity, as to the legitimacy and *reality* of colored Masons; and, consequently, a Committee from the Grand Lodge of Pennsylvania (white) was appointed to visit the colored Grand Lodge then situated in Eleventh Street, (Phila.) to apply the Masonic *test*, and *prove* or disprove their capacity as recipients of the ancient and honorable rituals of the mystic order.

A Grand Communication being congregated for the purpose, at the appointed time, the Committee went. A Committee of Examination being sent out, who—instead of as they should have done, had there been in waiting St. John the Baptist, St. John the Evangelist, or St. Paul in his daring *attitude* as the chief Christian on the Isle of Malta; *examined* them—on seeing the gentlemen, all men of the first standing in the city of Philadelphia, who had often been seen in Masonic processions, and so far, *known*—

as they thought—to be Masons—an unwise conclusion to be sure; reported them to the Chair; when without a question—and entirely through deference—the Chair replied, "Admit them," &c.—They entered; inspected, oversighted, and examined the work of the colored Masons, applying the scrutiny of a suspicious eye, and the test of plumb, level and square; all of which they pronounced to be good work, square, and just such work as was required to be done; but, for this act of *courte y*, and undue *defer ence* on their part, they were denounced by the Grand Lodge of Pennsylvania, as being unworthy of the high privileges they possessed.

Had these gentlemen been half so generous as they were determined on being just, they could and would have readily excused the blunder made by the colored Masons, when considering the relative position in community of the two parties who then met as Committees; the one subservient to the other in all the relations of life. In all the social relations in which they had formerly met, the one was domestic and the other superior—the one ignorant and the other intelligent; in a word, the one master and the other servant.

But, I come not to plead in extenuation for the blunders—the palpable and reprehensible blunders of our colored Masonic brethren and fathers; may I not say that it served them right, and has done them good, since their too great deference for persons in certain relations of life in this country, has done us much injury in other respects than this. But that time is not *now*, neither are *we* those brethren; and they who now stand at the head of our Masonic jurisdiction, are competent and adequate to the task for which they have been selected; so that the same excuse no longer exists for the Grand Lodge of Pennsylvania. Neither would I vindictively censure our fathers, as they did very well for their day and generation; and all that they did, was done for the best: they *meant* well, and that is all, at least, that I require at their hands. And now, in presence of this vast assemblage, before all the world, in the name of the Holy St. John—calling God to witness, I this day acquit them of all blame in the matter of that which they did, in admitting the Grand Lodge Visiting Committee, promising it will *never be done again!*

The second, and probably most formidable objection raised to colored Masons was, that they emanated from Grand Lodges, existing contrary to the general regulations of Masonry, in States where there were previously existing Grand Lodges.

This objection will easily be refuted, when it is considered that under the government of England, whence the general regulations of Masonry take their modern rise, for the sake of the craft, prompted by necessity, the establishment of a Grand Lodge was permitted in Scotland and Ireland; and at one time, for a short period, probably Wales; although the Grand Lodge of England extended her jurisdiction over all of these provinces.

At the time, the Scotch, Irish, and Welsh, all had certain domestic, social and political relations which seriously forbade their identity with the Grand Lodge of England; consequently, they severally established their own jurisdictions, all of which, were cordially acknowledged and sanctioned by the Grand Lodge of the British Empire. I may be mistaken about the Welsh; but as to the others, I am certain.*

*And even now, in consequence of the peculiar position and relations of the two places, there exists in the Canadas a Grand

And can there be a greater demand for an independent jurisdiction of Masonry among the Scotch and Irish than among the colored men of the United States? Certainly not. Nothing like so great; as among them, it was a matter of *choice*, not wishing, for reasons better known to themselves, to be subordinate to the Grand Lodge of England; while with us it was forced upon our fathers by *necessity*, they having applied to different Grand Lodges, at different times, in different States—as in Massachusetts and Pennsylvania—for warrants to work *under* them, and as often spurned and rejected. What could, what should, or what would they do but establish an independent jurisdiction? If they desired to be Masons, they must have done this; indeed, not to have done it, would have been to relinquish their rights as men, and certainly be less than Masons.

But we profess to be both men and Masons; and challenge the world, to try us, prove us, and disprove us, if they can.*

Lodge for the British Provinces of North America, extending over Nova Scotia, New Brunswick, Canada East, Canada West, and the Hudson Bay country; Sir Allen Napier Mac Nab, Knight Baronet, Right Worshipful Grand Master, with full power to grant warrants and establish Subordinate Lodges throughout British America. This Grand Lodge jurisdiction, was established, not to suit the conveniency of the Most Worshipful Grand Lodge of England, but the conveniency and *peculiar circumstances* of the people of British North America, who demanded the right, which was readily *conceded* by the Most Worshipful Grand Lodge, thereby *acknowledging* the *legality* of such separate jurisdictions, all within the same political and Masonic dependencies.

* The late Chief Justice, John Gibson,—as Col. J. S. of this city, a high Mason, will bear witness—when Grand Master of Pennsylvania, was known to acknowledge that the colored Masons of Pennsylvania were as legal as the whites, but intimated

As the *ultimum et unicum remedium*—the last and only remedy—a resort has been made to prove that colored men in the United States are *ineligible* to Masonic privileges. And among the many who have made this attack, none stand forth with a bolder front than the honorable *Jacob Brinkerhoof*, of Ohio, ex-member of Congress, who, in an elaborate oration delivered before the Masonic Fraternity of that State in 1850 or '51, on an occasion of a Communication of the Grand Lodge, declared that no man who ever had been, or the descendant of any who had been a *slave*, could ever be a *Mason*. This, coming from such authority, on such an occasion, was eagerly seized hold of, and published in the news journals from Baffin's Bay to Behring's Straits. It may have been sport to him, but certainly was intended as death to us; and the honorable ex-member of Congress, may yet learn, that he is much

that it would be "bad policy" so to decide publicly. Bad policy! *Policy* in *Masonry!* and *wrong* to do *right!* Cherubim shrink back from the portals of Mercy, drooping their golden pinions in sorrow; and Justice casts down her balance, and cases her sword in despair!

In 1847, after the establishment of Star Lodge No. 18, in Carlisle, Pa. a Committee of white Masons from the white Lodge in Carlisle—working under the Grand Lodge of Pennsylvania—with the Worshipful Master at its head, visited a Committee from the colored Lodge; and after a satisfactory conference, decided that they were *legal* and worthy ancient York Masons, but never, as they *promised*, made a report. The writer has met with white Masons who have been frank enough to tell him that they had been *obligated* not to recognize nor fellowship a *colored Mason!* These were *Pennsylvnnia* Masons. But he is frank to say, that while they are timid about *visiting*, there are hundreds who readily recognize a colored Mason wherever they *find* him, and consider it contrary to Masonry to act otherwise.

more of an adept in legal than Masonic jurisprudence—much better adapted to State than Lodge government. How will this bear the test of intelligent inquiry? Let us examine.

Moses, as before mentioned, of whom the highest enconium given, is said to have been *learned* in *all* the *wisdom* of the Egyptians, was not only the descendant of those who had been slaves, but of *slave parents;* and *himself, at the time* that he was so *taught* and *instructed* in this WISDOM, *was a slave!* Will it be denied that the man who appeared before Pharaoh, and was able to perform *mystically* all that the wisest among the wise men of that mysteriously wise nation were capable of doing, was a Mason? Was not the man who became the *Prime Minister* and *High Priest* of *Ceremonies* among the wise men of of Africa, a *Mason?* If so, will it be disputed that he was *legitimately* such? Are not we as Masons, and the world of mankind, to *him* the Egyptian *slave*—may I not add, the *fugitive* slave—indebted for a transmission to us of the Masonic Records—the Holy Bible, the Word of God? What says the honorable Jacob Brinkerhoof to this? Let a silent tongue answer the inquiry, and a listening ear give sanction to his condemnation.

But if this doctrine held good, according to the acceptation of the term *slave*, any one who has been deprived of his liberty, and thereby rendered politically and socially impotent, *is* a slave; and, consequently, Louis Kossuth, ex-Governor of Hungary, bound by the chains of Austria, in the city of Pateya, was, to all intents and purposes, according to this definition, a slave. And when he effected his escape to the United States, was (like Moses from Egypt) a fugitive slave from his masters in Austria, and, therefore, by the decree of the honorable ex-member of Congress, *incapable* of ever becoming a Mason.

But Governor Kossuth was made a Mason in Cincinnati, Ohio, the resident State of Mr. Brinkerhoof, and, therefore, according to him, the Governor is *not* a Mason at all. He *has been a slave!* Is the Order prepared for this? Is Mr. Brinkerhoof prepared for it? No, he is not. Then what becomes of his vaunting against colored men? for towards such he intended his declarations to have a bearing. Let the deserved rebuke of silence answer.

But was the requisition, that men should be *free born*, or *free at the time* of making them Masons, intended, morally and logically, to apply to those who lost their liberty by any force of invasion and unjust superior power?

No such thing. In the days of King Solomon, as mentioned elsewhere, there were two classes of men denied Masonic privileges: he who lost his liberty by crime, and he who, like Esau, "sold his birthright for a mess of pottage"—a class who bartered away their liberty for a term of years, in consideration of a trifling pecuniary gain. These persons were the same in condition as the Coolies (so called) in China, and the Peons of Mexico, both of whom voluntarily surrendered their rights, at discretion, to another. These persons, and these alone, were provided against, in the wise regulations concerning freemen, as Masons.

Did they apply to any others, the patriot, sage, warrior, chieftain and hero—indeed, the only true *brave* and chivalric, the most worthy and best specimens of mankind—would be denied a privilege, which, it would seem, they should be the most legitimate heirs.

The North American Indians, too, have been enslaved; and yet there has not, to my knowledge, been a syllable spoken or written against their legitimacy; and they, too, are Masons, or have Masonry among them, the facts of which are frequently referred to by white Masonic orators, with pleasurable approbation and pride.

But to deny to black men the privileges of Masonry, is to deny to a child the lineage of its own parentage. From whence sprung Masonry but from Ethiopia, Egypt, and Assyria—all settled and peopled by the children of Ham?

Does any one doubt the wisdom of Ethiopia? I have but to reply, that in the days of King Solomon's renown and splendor, she was capable of sending her *daughters* to prove him with hard questions. If this be true, what must have been her *sons!* A striking and important historical fact will be brought to bear, touching the truthfulness of this matter; and, discarding all profane and general, I shall take sacred history as our guide.

Moses was quite a young man—and, consequently, could not have been endowed with *wisdom*—when, seeing the maltreatment of an Israelite by the Egyptian, he slew him, burying his body in the sand; when, immediately after, the circumstance having become known to Pharaoh, he fled into Midian, a kingdom of Ethiopia.

He here sought the family of *Jethro*, the Ethiopian prince and Priest of Midian, in whose sight, after a short residence, he found favor, and married his daughter Zipporah. Zipporah, being a princes, was a shepherdess and priestess, as all priests were shepherds;* and Moses, con-

* It is frequently referred to by modern writers, as an evidence of the reverses of circumstances in the life of man, who, with some degree of surprise, tell us that king David was once a shepherd, and attended flocks. This is no strange matter, when it is remembered that all princes in those days were *priests;* and *all*

sequently, became a shepherd, keeping the flocks of Jethro his father-in law, watching them by day and by night, on hill and in valley. Here Moses continued to dwell, until called by the message of the Lord, to sue before Pharaoh for the deliverance of Israel.

From whence could Moses—he leaving Egypt when young—have derived his wisdom, if not from the Ethiopians? Is it not a reasonable, nay, the only just conclusion to infer, that his deep seated knowledge was received from them, and that his learned wife Zipporah, who accompanied him by day and by night, through hills and vales, contributed not a little to his acquirements? Certainly, this must have been so; for the Egyptians were a colony from Ethiopia, and derived their first training from them; the former, as the country filled up, moving and spreading farther down the Nile, until, at length, becoming very numerous, they separated the kingdom, establishing an independent nation, occupying the delta at the mouths of the river.

Where could there a place, so appropriate be found, for

priests, as a necessary part of their education, had to be *shepherds.* As we may reasonably infer, there were two objects in view in the establishment of this singular mythological ordinance. The first was, that the shepherd, by continually looking out for a change of weather, and thereby gazing up to the heavens, might keep his mind more fixed upon the high calling that awaited him—administering at the altar—and thus assimilate the person of his deity; and the second, that by attending the sheep, he might be impressed with their *innocence,* and thereby learn the true character that should distinguish him before the gaze of the inquisitive eye. Of the seven *daughters of Midian,* the children of Jethro, all, as will be seen, were shepherdesses, and, consequently, all priestesses. Ex. 2 c.

the study of those mysteries as upon the *highest hills* and in the *deepest valleys?* Is it not thus that the mysteries originated, the habits of the shepherds with their flocks, leading them to the hills and valleys?

It was also in Ethiopia where God appeared to Moses in a *burning bush;* and here where he told him, "Put off thy shoes from off thy feet; for the place whereon t' standeth is *holy ground.*" And this "holy ground' was in Ethiopia or Midian, the true ancient Africa. Truly, if the African race have no legitimate claims to Masonry, then is it illegitimate to all the rest of mankind.

Upon this topic I shall not farther descant, as I believe it is a settled and acknowledged fact, conceded by all *intelligent* writers and speakers, that to Africa is the world indebted for its knowledge of the mysteries of Ancient Freemasonry. Had Moses, nor the Israelites, never lived in Africa, the mysteries of the wise men of the East had never been handed down to us.

Was it not Africa that gave birth to Euclid, the master geometrician of the world? and was it not in consequence of a twenty-five years' residence in Africa, that the great Pythagorus was enabled to discover that key problem in geometry—the forty-seventh problem of Euclid—without which Masonry would be incomplete? Must I hesitate to tell the world that, as applied to Masonry, the word—*Eureka*—was first exclaimed in Africa? But—there! I have revealed the Masonic *secret*, and *must stop!*

Masons, Brethren, Companions and Sir Knights, hoping that for this disclosure, by a slip of the tongue, you will forgive me—as I may have made the world much wiser—I now commit you and our cause into the care and keeping of the Grand Master of the Universe.

9 781169 543515